$37^2 = [(3)(37 + 7)]\,(7^2)$

$= (132)(49)$

$= 1369$

Therefore, the square root of **37** is **1369**.

$90 \div 5$

VEDIC MATHS

$\dfrac{100}{50}$

$33^2 = 1089$

WORKBOOK 4

13^2

Om KIDZ

An imprint of **Om** Books International

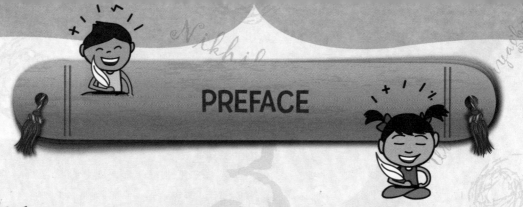

PREFACE

Vedic Mathematics is an ancient system of Mathematics. It was rediscovered from the Vedas by Swami Bharati Krishna Tirtha between 1911 and 1918. Vedic Mathematics is based on 16 sutras or word formulae. By using these formulae, the mind can be trained to solve mathematical problems with greater ease and accuracy.

Vedic Mathematics helps making mental calculations easier. It is a flexible system wherein the students have the liberty of inventing their own methods of calculations. This results in the calculations becoming much faster than regular methods. This enhances the students' interest in Mathematics.

The **Om Vedic Maths Workbook series** (Level 1 to Level 4) focuses on basic mathematical concepts such as addition, subtraction, multiplication and division that are explained in a fun and easy-to-understand manner. These books will cover the following four sutras:

Digital root: Navashesh

All from 9 and the last from 10: Nikhilam

Vertically and cross-wise: Urdhva-Tiryagbhyam

One less than the previous one: Ekanyunena Purvena

The remainder by the last digit: Sheshanyankena Charamena

One more than previous one: Ekadhikena Purvena

Transpose and adjust: Paravartya Yojayet

The concepts of Vedic Mathematics are easy to understand, apply and remember. This book aims at developing an interest in Mathematics and making the subject easy and fun. It also aims at sharpening the student's mind and increase accuracy as well. This in turn will increase the student's concentration and logical thinking.

GENERAL FORMULA FOR SQUARING OF NUMBERS

This general formula allows you to square any number instantly! Follow this rule:

Say the number is D1D2

$$(D1D2)^2 = [(D1)\ (D1D2 + D2)]\ (D2)^2$$

Example 1: Find the square of **23**.

Here, D1 = 2, D2 = 3 and D1D2 = 23

> Using the formula:
> $(D1D2)^2 = [(D1)\ (D1D2 + D2)]\ (D2)^2$

$$23^2 = [(2)(23 + 3)]\ (3^2)$$
$$= (52)(9)$$
$$= 529$$

Therefore, the square of **23** is **529**.

Example 2: Find the square of **37**.

Here, D1 = 3, D2 = 7 and D1D2 = 37

> Using the formula:
> $(D1D2)^2 = [(D1)\ (D1D2 + D2)]\ (D2)^2$

$$37^2 = [(3)(37 + 7)]\ (7^2)$$
$$= (132)(49)$$
$$= 1369 \quad \text{Keep 9 and carry over 4 to 132.}$$

Therefore, the square root of **37** is **1369**.

Find the squares of the following numbers.

1 $13^2 =$

2 $27^2 =$

3 $49^2 =$

Use this space for your calculations.

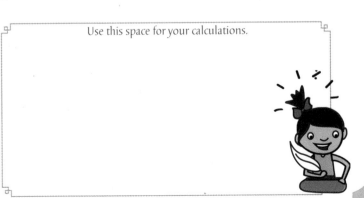

4   56^2 =

5   74^2 =

6   85^2 =

7   96^2 =

8   91^2 =

9   51^2 =

10 17^2 =

11 18^2 =

12 29^2 =

13 88^2 =

14 46^2 =

VERTICAL METHOD FOR SQUARING OF NUMBERS

This is an easier method for squaring numbers.
Follow this rule:
Say the number is D1D2
$(D1D2)^2 = [(D1)^2] [2D1D2] [(D2)^2]$

Example 1: Find the square of **24**.

Here, D1 = 2, D2 = 4 and D1D2 = 24.

$24^2 = [2^2] [2 \times 2 \times 4] [4^2]$

$= [4] [16] [16]$

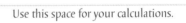
Using the formula:
$(D1D2)2 = [(D1)^2][2D1D2][(D2)^2]$

$= 576$

Therefore, the square of **24** is **576**.

Find the squares of the following numbers.

1   32^2 =

2   45^2 =

3   69^2 =

4   87^2 =

5   46^2 =

6   37^2 =

Use this space for your calculations.

7 29^2 =

8 25^2 =

9 64^2 =

10 93^2 =

11 81^2 =

12 84^2 =

13 54^2 =

14 73^2 =

15 28^2 =

16 19^2 =

Use this space for your calculations.

SQUARING OF NUMBERS BY BOX METHOD

You have already learnt the box method for multiplication. Did you know you can use the same method to square the numbers. Follow this rule:

Consider a two-digit number D1D2.

The square of a two-digit number will be a four-digit number.

Follow the box method. Add diagonally to arrive at the answer.

X	D1	D2
D1	D1 x D1	D1 x D2
D2	D1 x D2	D2 x D2

Example 1: Find the square of **54**.

X	5	4
5	2 / 5	2 / 0
4	2 / 0	1 / 6

Add diagonally.

The square of 54 is a four-digit number, that is, A1, A2, A3, A4. Add diagonally to arrive at answer.

Therefore, **A1 = 2**

A2 = 2 + 5 + 2 = 9

A3 = 0 + 1 + 0 = 1

A4 = 6

Arranging the digits,

A1A2A3A4 = 2916

So, **54 × 54 = 2916**

Find the squares of the following numbers.

1 67^2 =

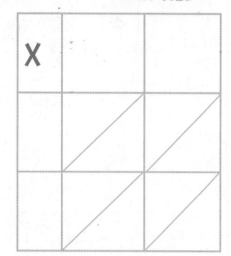

2 98^2 =

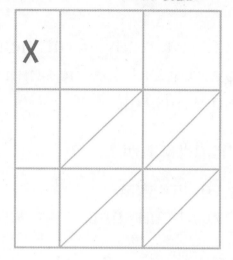

3 43^2 =

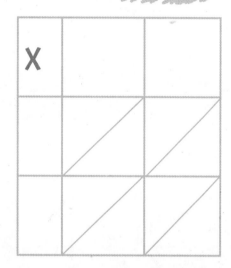

4 90^2 =

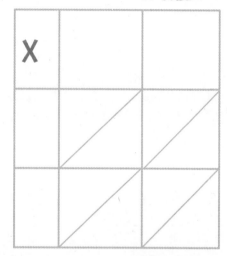

5 76^2 =

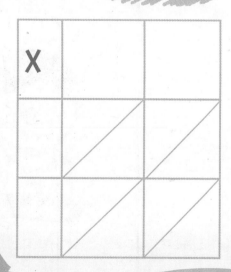

6 87^2 =

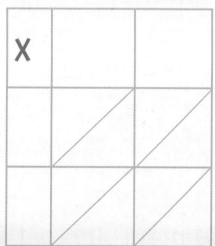

7 154² =

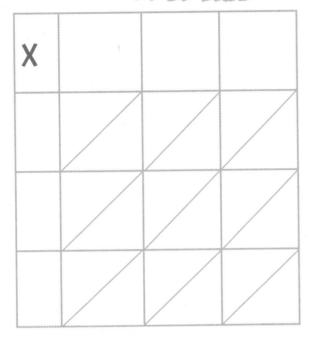

8 342² =

9 423² =

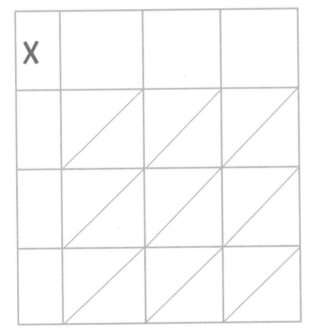

10 276² =

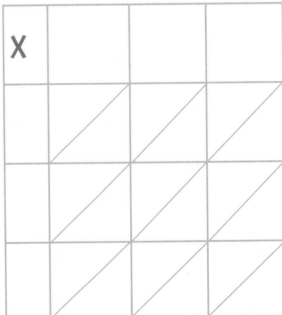

Use this space for your calculations.

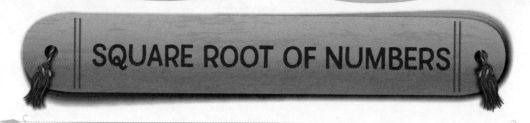

SQUARE ROOT OF NUMBERS

If you know the square roots of all the numbers up to 10 and the Nikhilam sutra, you can find the square root of the other numbers easily.

This is how to do it:
- Divide the given number into two parts, taking pairs from the right hand side.
- A three-digit number will be (D1) (D2D3).
- A four-digit number will be (D1D2) (D3D4).
- Find the nearest possible square of the number in the first column. That will be the first part of the answer. The last part depends on the last digit in the given number.

If last digit of number is:	Then last digit of square root will be:
1	1 or 9
4	2 or 8
5	5
6	4 or 6
9	3 or 7
0	0

Example 1: Find the square root of **7056**.

7056 ← Here, divide the number into parts, that is, (D1D2) (D3D4).

Step 1: The nearest square to 70 is 64 (square of 8). So, the first part of the answer is **8**.

Step 2: The last digit in the number is 6. So, the last digit in the square root can be either **4** or **6**.

Step 3: Putting the digits in step 1 and step 2 together, the square root is either **84** or **86**.

Step 4: Find the square of 84 and 86 to find out which one is the correct answer.

Step 5: Here, the square root is **84**.

___

Example 2: Find the square root of **15376**.

15376

Here, divide the number into two, that is, (D1D2D3) (D4D5).

Step 1: The nearest square to 153 is 144 (square of 12). So, the first part of the answer is **12**.

Step 2: The last digit in the number is 6. So, the last digit in the square root can either be **4** or **6**.

Step 3: Putting the digits in step 1 and step 2 together, the square root is either **124** or **126**.

Step 4: Find the square of 124 and 126 to find out which one is the correct answer.

Step 5: Here, the square root is **124**.

Find the square roots of the following numbers.

Use this space for your calculations.

1   289 =

2   361 =

3   484 =

4   625 =

5   841 =

6 2025 =

7 3364 =

8 6084 =

9 5329 =

10 9801 =

11 3249 =

12 3969 =

13 7056 =

14 17956 =

15 24336 =

16 12321 =

17 10201 =

Use this space for your calculations.

CUBES OF NUMBERS CLOSE TO 100

Cubes of numbers can be obtained using the Yavdunam Sutra.

- Step 1: To find the cube of a three-digit number closer to 100, take base as 100. Find out the excess over 100. For example, if the number is 106, the excess over 100 is 106 – 100 = 6.

- Step 2: Then, double this excess and add it to the original number. Here, the excess being 6, double of 6 is 12, so add 12 to original number 106, that is, get 106 + 12 = 118. This becomes the left-hand portion of the answer. Also, the new excess now is 118 – 100 = 18.

- Step 3: Multiply first excess with new excess. Here, it is 6 x 18 = 108. This is the middle portion of the answer.

- Step 4: To find last portion of the answer, find the cube of the original excess, that is, 6 (cube is 216).

- Step 5: Arrange everything together and carry over wherever necessary. The three parts of answer are 118 108 216.

Carry over

$$118 \quad 108 \quad 216$$
$$\underline{\quad 1 \quad \quad 2 \quad}$$

The answer is: 1 1 9 1 0 1 6

Example : Find the cube of **112**.

Step 1: Excess of 112 over base 100 = 112 – 100 = 12

Step 2: Double the excess, that is, 12 x 2 = 24; add the product to the original number, that is, 112 + 24 = 136. The left-hand side digits are 136. New excess = **36**.

Step 3: Old excess x new excess = 12 x 36 = 432. **432** is the middle portion of the answer.

Step 4: Cube of original excess 12 = 12^3 = 1728. **1728** is the last portion of the answer.

Step 5: Write all the parts together and carry over wherever required.

136   432   1728
           17   28

Keep 28 carry over 17.

The number of digits taken from the last answer should always be 1 less than the number of digits in the number whose cube is being found.

449 28
4   49 28
_____
140 49 28

Keep 49 carry over 4.

Hence cube of **112** is **1404928**.

Find the cubes of the following numbers.

1. 113^3 =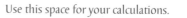

2. 127^3 =

3. 106^3 =

4. 119^3 =

5. 114^3 =

6. 111^3 =

7. 134^3 =

8. 128^3 =

9. 107^3 =

10. 140^3 =

Use this space for your calculations.

GENERAL METHOD FOR CUBING NUMBERS

The Anurupya sutra can be used to find the cubes of numbers. If you know the cubes of numbers 1 to 9, this formula is an easy way to find the cubes of any given number.

To find the cube of $D1D2^3$

Find: $D1^3$, $D1^2D2$, $D1D2^2$, $D2^3$, then arrange as follows:

$$D1D2^3 = D1^3 + D1^2D2 + D1D2^2 + D2^3$$
$$2D1^2D2 \quad 2D1D2^2$$

Example : Find the cube of **15**.

$D1^3 = 1^3 = 1$

$D2^3 = 5^3 = 125$

$D1^2D2 = 1 \times 1 \times 5 = 5$

$D1D2^2 = 1 \times 5 \times 5 = 25$

$2D1^2D2 = 10$

$2D1D2^2 = 50$

$$
\begin{array}{r}
15^3 = 1 \quad\; 5 \quad 25 \;\; 125 \\
10 \quad 50 \quad\;\; \\
2 \quad\;\; 8 \quad 12 \quad\;\; \\
\hline
3 \quad\;\; 3 \quad\;\; 7 \quad\;\; 5 \\
\end{array}
$$

Carry forwards

Hence cube of **15** is **3375**.

Find the cubes of the following numbers.

Use this space for your calculations.

1 11^3 =

2 14^3 =

3 17^3 =

4 18^3 =

5 21^3 =

6 27^3 =

7 35^3 =

8 39^3 =

9 90^3 =

10 118^3 =

11 212^3 =

12 541^3 =

13 612^3 =

14 110^3 =

Use this space for your calculations.

16

WORD PROBLEMS

Use all the new methods you have learnt to solve the following word problems.

1. A museum has 16 crowns, each with 16 gemstone flowers. Each gemstone flower has 16 gemstones. How many gemstones are there in the museum?

2. 15 girls have 15 sacks each. Each sack contains 15 apples. How many apples are there in all?

3. There are 12 crates of 12 dozen eggs. How many eggs are there in all?

CUBE ROOTS OF NUMBERS

Finding cube roots is not tedious and difficult anymore! To find cube roots of any number, you should know the cubes of single-digit numbers.

Cubes	Last Digits	Cubes	Last Digits
$1^3 = 1$	1	$6^3 = 216$	6
$2^3 = 8$	8	$7^3 = 343$	3
$3^3 = 27$	7	$8^3 = 512$	2
$4^3 = 64$	4	$9^3 = 729$	9
$5^3 = 125$	5		

Did you notice that there is no overlapping as was the case for squares of numbers.

Step 1: Group the digits in sets of three, starting from the right-hand side. Example: 1723 = (1) (723); 85184 = (85) (184); 729000 = (729) (000)
Number of digits in the cube root will be equal to number of groups formed.

Step 2: The first group decides the first number of the cube root by mere inspection.

Step 3: The last digit of the number determines the last digit of the cube root.

Example: Find cube root of **226981**.

Step 1: Dividing the number into groups of 3.

226|981 ← Two groups means the answer will have two digits.

Step 2: The first part of the answer is 226, the closest number cube to **226** is **6** ($6^3 = 216$). Hence, the first portion of the answer is **6**.

Step 3: The second portion of the answer is **1**, because the last digit of the number is **1**.

Hence cube root of **226981** is **61**.

Find the cube roots of the following numbers.

① **8000** =

② **6859** =

③ **4913** =

④ **3375** =

⑤ **2197** =

Use this space for your calculations.

⑥ **1728** =

7 74088 =

8 59319 =

9 46656 =

10 27000 =

11 85184 =

12 103823 =

13 314432 =

14 857375 =

15 205379 =

16 421875 =

Use this space for your calculations.

FRACTIONS TO DECIMALS

Learn to express a fraction as a decimal, to all its decimal places. Follow the Sutra of "Remainders by the last digit". This sutra is used to make calculations with very high levels of accuracy.

Example : Express $\dfrac{1}{8}$ as decimal.

Step 1: Add a 0 to the one's place. Now, the numerator becomes 10 instead of 1.

$\dfrac{10}{8}$

Step 2: If this number is less than the denominator, add another 0, or else proceed to step 3.

Step 3: Divide the number by the denominator and find the quotient and remainder. Here, Q = 1 R = 2

Step 4: Add a 0 to the remainder and divide it by the denominator. So, Q = 2 R = 4

$\dfrac{20}{8}$

Step 5: Repeat step 4. Add a 0 to the new remainder and divide by the denominator. So Q = 5 R = 0

$\dfrac{40}{8}$

Step 6: Write all the quotients obtained in order from step 3 onwards. Here they are: 1, 2, 5

Step 7: Now, write all the numbers together with a 0 and decimal point before them.

Step 8: So, $\dfrac{1}{8} = 0.125$

Note: If, instead of '0' the remainder at some point is the same as the numerator, we stop there. This is because the answer is going to repeat from there on.

For example $\dfrac{1}{7} = 0.142857142857$

1. $\dfrac{1}{5}$ =

2. $\dfrac{1}{4}$ =

3. $\dfrac{1}{6}$ =

4. $\dfrac{1}{9}$ =

5. $\dfrac{1}{7}$ =

6. $\dfrac{2}{7}$ =

7. $\dfrac{1}{8}$ =

8. $\dfrac{2}{9}$ =

9. $\dfrac{3}{8}$ =

10. $\dfrac{3}{4}$ =

SERIES

Sometimes, we notice a pattern while solving mathematical problems. Based on this pattern, we can create a series.

A. If 33^2 $=$ 1089

333^2 $=$ 110889

3333^2 $=$ 11108889

Find the hidden pattern and complete the series:

1 33333^2 $=$

2 333333^2 $=$

3 3333333^2 $=$

4 33333333^2 $=$

5 333333333^2 $=$

B. If 66^2 $=$ 4356

666^2 $=$ 443556

6666^2 $=$ 44435556

Find the hidden pattern and complete the series:

1 66666^2 $=$

2   666666^2 =

3   6666666^2 =

4   66666666^2 =

5   666666666^2 =

C. If 99^2 =   9801

999^2 =   998001

9999^2 =   99980001

Find the hidden pattern and complete the series:

1   99999^2 =

2   999999^2 =

3   9999999^2 =

4   99999999^2 =

5   999999999^2 =

D. If   1   ✕   1   =   1

11   ✕   11   =   121

111   ✕   111   =   12321

1111   ✕   1111   =   1234321

Find the hidden pattern and complete the series:

1. 11111 ✖ 11111 = ▨▨▨▨

2. 111111 ✖ 111111 = ▨▨▨▨

3. 1111111 ✖ 1111111 = ▨▨▨▨

4. 11111111 ✖ 11111111 = ▨▨▨▨

5. 111111111 ✖ 111111111 = ▨▨▨▨

E. If 9 ✖ 9 + 9 = 90

99 ✖ 99 + 99 = 9900

999 ✖ 999 + 999 = 999000

Complete the series upto 999999999 x 999999999 + 999999999

SOLVING SIMPLE EQUATIONS

Solving algebraic equations involves a lot of cross-multiplication and tedious calculations. However, Vedic math allows us to solve simple equations practically by mere observation!

Equations can be in various forms. You will learn how to solve each one by using a sutra called 'Sunyam Samysamuccaye' or 'equal to zero'. According to this sutra, the common element in an equation must be determined and is equated to a zero.

Example 1: Where there is a common factor on both sides:

$$3(x+2)+(x+2)=5(x+2)$$

Here, the common factor is (x + 2). Instead of solving it the usual way, equate the common element (x +2) to 0.

So, $x+2=0$; $x=-2$ is the solution

Example 2: Where the product of the independent terms on both sides is same:

$$(x+4)(x+5)=(x+2)(x+10)$$

Here, notice that the product of the independent terms 4 and 5 on the left-hand side is 20 and also the product of 2 and 10 is 20.
In such cases, we can directly say the solution will be x = 0

Example 3: Where the numerical value of the numerator is same.

$$\frac{1}{3x+1}+\frac{1}{2x+1}=0$$

In such cases, equate the sum of the denominators to 0.
Here, 3x +1 + 2x +1 = 5x + 2
Equate this to 0 directly:

$$5x+2=0 \ ; \ 5x=-2; \ x=\frac{-2}{5}$$

26

$$\frac{1}{x-1} + \frac{1}{x-2} = \frac{1}{x-1} + \frac{1}{x-4}$$

In such cases, equate the sum of the denominators to 0.
Here again, the sum of denominators on the left-hand side =
$(x-1) + (x-2) = 2x-3$
and the sum of denominators on the right-hand side =
$(x-1) + (x-4) = 2x-5$

So we equate $2x-5$ to 0 ; $2x-5=0$; $2x=5$; $x = \frac{5}{2}$

Example 4: Where the sum of the numerators and the sum of the denominators is the same.

$$\frac{3x+2}{3x+3} = \frac{3x+4}{3x+3}$$

Here, observe that $3x + 2 + 3x + 4 = 6x + 6$
and $3x + 3 + 3x + 3 = 6x + 6$
Equating this to zero: $6x + 6 = 0$; $6x = -6$; $x = -1$

Equating this to zero: $6x - 6 = 0$; $6x = -6$; $x = -1$

Note: Sometimes, the common element may not be apparent immediately. Some modification may be required to obtain it.

Solve the following equations using the tricks you have just learnt.

1. $7(x+2) + 4(x+2) = 5(x+2)$

2 $4(x + 1) + 4(x + 1) = 6(x + 1)$

3 $(x + 6)(x + 5) = (x + 15)(x + 2)$

4 $\dfrac{1}{6x + 1} + \dfrac{1}{5x + 1} = 0$

5 $\dfrac{4x + 12}{3x + 6} = \dfrac{3x + 4}{4x + 10}$

SOLVING SIMULTANEOUS EQUATIONS

Solving simultaneous equations again involves a lot of cross-multiplication calculations. However, Vedic maths allows us to solve these with a simple trick!

Follow the rules:

Step 1: Find the difference between the (coefficient of y in the first equation x constant in the second equation) and (coefficient of y in the second equation x constant in the first equation).

Step 2: Find the difference between the (coefficient of y in the first equation x coefficient of x in the second equation) and (coefficient of y in the second equation coefficient of x in the first equation).

Step 3: Value of x will be $\dfrac{\text{Answer from step 1}}{\text{Answer from step 2}}$

Step 4: Simply substitute this value of x to find y.

Example: Solve:
$$4x + 2y = 10$$
$$6x - 8y = 4$$

Step 1: Find the difference between the (co-efficient of y in the first equation x constant in the second equation) and (co-efficient of y in the second equation x constant in the first equation).

$$(2 \times 4) - (-8 \times 10) = 8 + 80 = 88$$

Step 2: Find the difference between the (co-efficient of y in the first equation x co-efficient of x in the second equation) – (co-efficient of y in the second equation x co-efficient of x in the first equation)

$$(2 \times 6) - (-8 \times 4) = 12 + 32 = 44$$

Step 3: Value of x will be $\dfrac{\text{Answer from step 1}}{\text{Answer from step 2}}$

$$x = \frac{88}{44} = 2$$

Step 4: Simply substitute this value of x to find y.
In equation 1 putting x=2 we get:

$$4\,(2) + 2y = 10;\ 2y = 10 - 8;\ 2y = 2;\ y = 1$$

So solution is $x = 2;\ y = 1$

Solve the following simultaneous equations in less than a minute.

1 $3x - 2y = 2;\ 2x + y = 5$

2 $2x - 2y = 14;\ 10x + 4y = 84$

3 $10x - 6y = 22;\ 12x - 10y = 18$

4 $6x - 4y = 55; 4x - 6y = 35$

5 $36x + 24y = 21; 48x - 48y = 42$

6 $2x + y = 5; 3x - 4y = 2$

ANSWERS

Page 3 and 4
1.	169	8.	8281
2.	729	9.	2601
3.	2401	10.	289
4.	3136	11.	324
5.	5476	12.	841
6.	7225	13.	7744
7.	9216	14.	2116

Page 5 and 6
1.	1024	9.	4096
2.	2025	10.	8649
3.	4761	11.	6561
4.	7569	12.	7056
5.	2116	13.	2916
6.	1369	14.	5329
7.	841	15.	784
8.	625	16.	361

Page 8 and 9
1.	4489	6.	7569
2.	9604	7.	23716
3.	1849	8.	116964
4.	8100	9.	178929
5.	5776	10.	76176

Page 11 and 12
1.	17	10.	99
2.	19	11.	57
3.	22	12.	63
4.	25	13.	84
5.	29	14.	134
6.	45	15.	156
7.	58	16.	111
8.	78	17.	101
9.	73		

Page 14
1.	1442897	6.	1367631
2.	2048383	7.	2406104
3.	1191016	8.	2097152
4.	1685159	9.	1225043
5.	1481544	10.	2744000

Page 15 and 16
1.	1331	8.	59319
2.	2744	9.	729000
3.	4913	10.	1643032
4.	5832	11.	9528128
5.	9261	12.	158340421
6.	19683	13.	229220928
7.	42875	14.	1331000

Page 17
1. 4096 gemstones
2. 3375 apples
3. 1728 eggs

Page 19 and 20
1.	20	9.	36
2.	19	10.	30
3.	17	11.	44
4.	15	12.	47
5.	13	13.	68
6.	12	14.	95
7.	42	15.	59
8.	39	16.	75

Page 22
1.	0.2	6.	0.285714
2.	0.25	7.	0.125
3.	0.1666666	8.	0.2222
4.	0.11111	9.	0.375
5.	0.142857	10.	0.75

Page 23, 24 and 25
A.
1. 1111088889
2. 111110888889
3. 11111108888889
4. 1111111088888889
5. 111111110888888889

B.
1. 4444355556
2. 444443555556
3. 44444435555556

4. 4444444355555556
5. 444444443555555556

C.
1. 9999800001
2. 999998000001
3. 99999980000001
4. 9999999800000001
5. 999999998000000001

D.
1. 123454321
2. 12345654321
3. 1234567654321
4. 123456787654321
5. 12345678987654321

E.
1. 99990000
2. 9999900000
3. 999999000000
4. 99999990000000
5. 9999999900000000
6. 999999999000000000

Page 27 and 28
1.	X = –2	4.	X = 2/11
2.	X = –1	5.	X = –16/7
3.	X = 0		

Page 30 and 31
1. X = –12/7; y = 11/7
2. X = 8; y = 2
3. X = 4; y = 3
4. X = 57/6; y = 1/2
5. X = 7/10; y = –7/40
6. X = 2; y = 1